Learning to Read
with
Vowels and Phonics

● Includes Fun Activities and Sight Words ●

By
Titilope Adegbemle

Text Copyright © 2024 by Titilope Adegbemle

All rights reserved. No part of this publication may be reproduced, stored in a retrieval system, or transmitted in any form or by any means—electronic, mechanical, photocopying, recording, or otherwise—without prior written permission from the publisher.

For permission requests, please visit www.skillfulreader.com.

Published by Skillful Reader

Austin, Texas

www.skillfulreader.com

Publisher's Cataloging-in-Publication Data

Names: Adegbemle, Titilope, author.
Title: Learning to Read with Vowels and Phonics / Titilope Adegbemle.
Description: Austin, TX: Skillful Reader, 2024. Summary: An engaging literacy book designed to help children learn how to read through phonics, letter blending, decoding words, and interactive activities.
Identifiers: LCCN: 2024911654 | ISBN: 978-1-964198-01-9 (Hardcover) | 978-1-964198-00-2 (Paperback) | 978-1-964198-02-6 (Epub)
Subjects: LCSH Readers (Primary) | Reading (Primary) | Reading--Phonetic method--Juvenile literature. | English language--Phonetics--Juvenile literature. | BISAC JUVENILE NONFICTION / Readers / Beginner | EDUCATION / Teaching / Subjects / Reading & Phonics
Classification: LCC PE1165 .A34 Le 2024 | DDC 421/.1--dc23

Dedication

To my husband and children - I couldn't have done it without you.

Table of Contents

Introduction	4
Why is Reading Important?	5
Methods to Encourage Children to Read Frequently	6
Vowels	9
Consonants	10
Alphabet	11
Phonics Chart	12
Blending Words	17
Consonant Vowel (CV) Blending - Short Vowel Aa	18
Consonant Vowel Consonant (CVC) Blending - Short Vowel Aa	19
Activities	20
Consonant Vowel (CV) Blending - Short Vowel Ee	21
Consonant Vowel Consonant (CVC) Blending - Short Vowel Ee	22
Activities	23
Consonant Vowel (CV) Blending - Short Vowel Ii	24
Consonant Vowel Consonant (CVC) Blending - Short Vowel Ii	25
Activities	26
Consonant Vowel (CV) Blending - Short Vowel Oo	27
Consonant Vowel Consonant (CVC) Blending - Short Vowel Oo	28
Activities	29
Consonant Vowel (CV) Blending - Short Vowel Uu	30
Consonant Vowel Consonant (CVC) Blending - Short Vowel Uu	31
Activities	32
Long Vowels	33
Long Vowel Words and Activities	34
Comparing Short and Long Vowel Words	44
Sight Words	46
Activities	48

 # Introduction

This book is a product of my passion for children and literacy. During the COVID-19 lockdown, I had the chance to teach reading and writing skills to my younger child. When a parent at the park asked about my methods and materials, it inspired me to turn my notes into a book. I recognize that reading is a fundamental skill essential for a successful life, and I aim to help parents who are struggling to teach their children to read.

This book uses the synthetic phonics approach, which begins by teaching letter sounds and gradually progresses to blending them to pronounce words. It starts with blending consonants and vowels (CV) and then moves on to blending consonant-vowel-consonant patterns (CVC) to form complete words.

Research has shown that the synthetic phonics approach significantly enhances reading accuracy, comprehension, spelling, and writing proficiency (Johnston & Watson, 2005). It also equips learners with the skills to decode unfamiliar words, recognize common spelling patterns, and grasp the underlying structure of the English language.

Moreover, synthetic phonics offers a structured and systematic approach, which is particularly advantageous for struggling readers and individuals with dyslexia. It features vibrant pictures, straightforward, easy-to-follow text, and activity worksheets, ensuring children have a fun and engaging reading experience.

Why is Reading Important?

Reading encourages language skills from an early age - as early as infancy. There are several benefits to children reading early, including expression, connection, association, understanding, and development. There are many studies that support the idea that teaching children to read will benefit them later in life. Reading is not just what you see on a page.

It is part of a bigger concept that incorporates phonemic awareness (sounds), phonics (letter-sound connection), fluency (speaking), comprehension (understanding), and writing. Reading is found across every area of life, and when a child begins reading early (though sometimes it may not be easy), it will set them up for success in the future.

Methods to Encourage Children to Read Frequently

If we want children to develop strong reading skills, we need to encourage them to read extensively. Beyond just wanting them to read well, our goal is to nurture their ability and inclination to read independently. This ensures they can easily access information and enjoy reading outside of school. The interdependence of these factors is crucial. To promote extensive reading among children, we must first ensure they are proficient readers (Adams, 1990). Here are ways to teach and encourage children to read regularly.

1 · Start Early:

Reading can be initiated from the very first few months of your child's life. Even infants can benefit from you reading to them because it exposes them to the rhythm and melody of language. Choose books with rhymes, poems, and songs that are engaging for your child.

2 • Read Aloud Together:

Regular read-aloud sessions with your child will help them hear themselves and refine their pronunciation. Choose repetitive books tailored to their interests and age and encourage them to help you read the parts they know (or have memorized), as this is the beginning stage of reading. As your child gets older, begin to encourage them to read a page and then you read a page.

3 • Use Phonics:

Introduce phonics to establish the connection between sounds and letters. This will help children understand the relationship between letters and their sounds and decode unknown words.

4 • Make Mistakes:

Show your child that it is okay to make mistakes. Mess up a word or say something that might not make sense. Then correct yourself and go back to reread. This helps children see that everyone makes mistakes, and there's no reason to be ashamed or embarrassed. Play it off, fix it, and move on.

5 • Be Patient and Supportive:

Be aware that every child progresses at their own pace. Be patient and supportive and understand their unique learning style. Celebrate small successes, such as learning a new letter sound or reading a high-frequency word, and offer encouragement throughout their reading journey.

6 · Encourage Writing:

Support your child in creating their own stories or keeping a journal. Writing improves reading skills and allows children to express themselves creatively. Remember that writing begins early with scribbles, lines, and shapes. Encourage your child to draw pictures, label them, and then begin to write words and sentences.

7 · Visit the Library:

Regular visits to the library can expose your child to a wide range of books and reading materials. Encouraging your child to explore books that interest them and allowing them to choose their own books can help them look forward to reading. Many local libraries also offer reading programs and storytelling sessions for children.

Remember that adopting a love for reading is as significant as teaching the mechanics of reading. Creating a positive and enjoyable reading experience will go a long way in developing a lifelong appreciation for books and learning.

Vowels

A vowel is a letter that represents an open sound. There are six vowels in the English language: a, e, i, o, u, and sometimes y.

There are short and long vowels, but this book will focus primarily on short vowels.

Consonants

A consonant is a speech sound that is not a vowel.

B C D F G H J
K L M N P Q R
S T V W X Y Z

Alphabet

Aa	Bb	Cc	Dd	Ee	Ff
Gg	Hh	Ii	Jj	Kk	Ll
Mm	Nn	Oo	Pp	Qq	Rr
Ss	Tt	Uu	Vv	Ww	Xx
Yy	Zz				

Phonics Chart

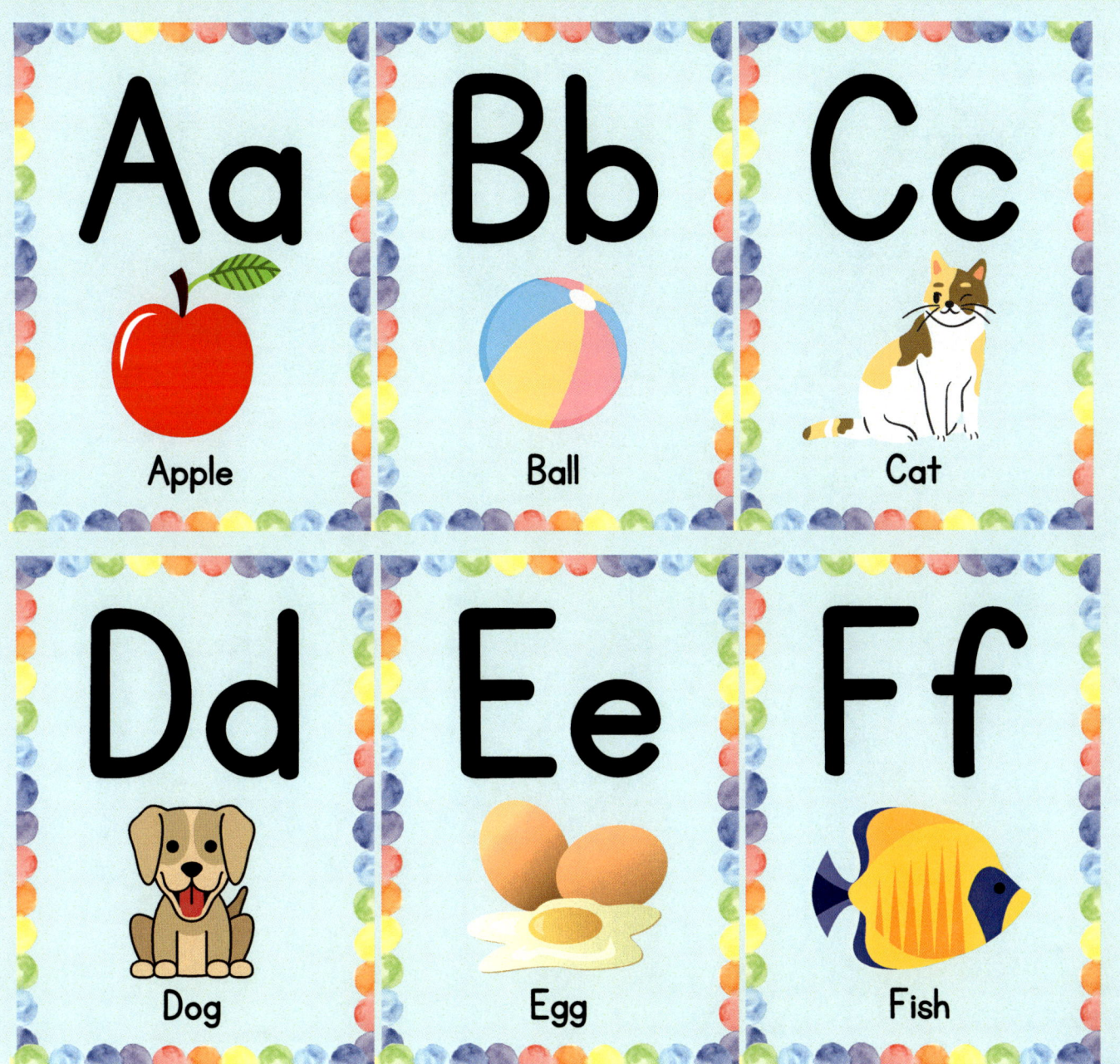

Gg	Hh	Ii
Goat	Hat	Ice cream
Jj	Kk	Ll
Jug	Kite	Lion

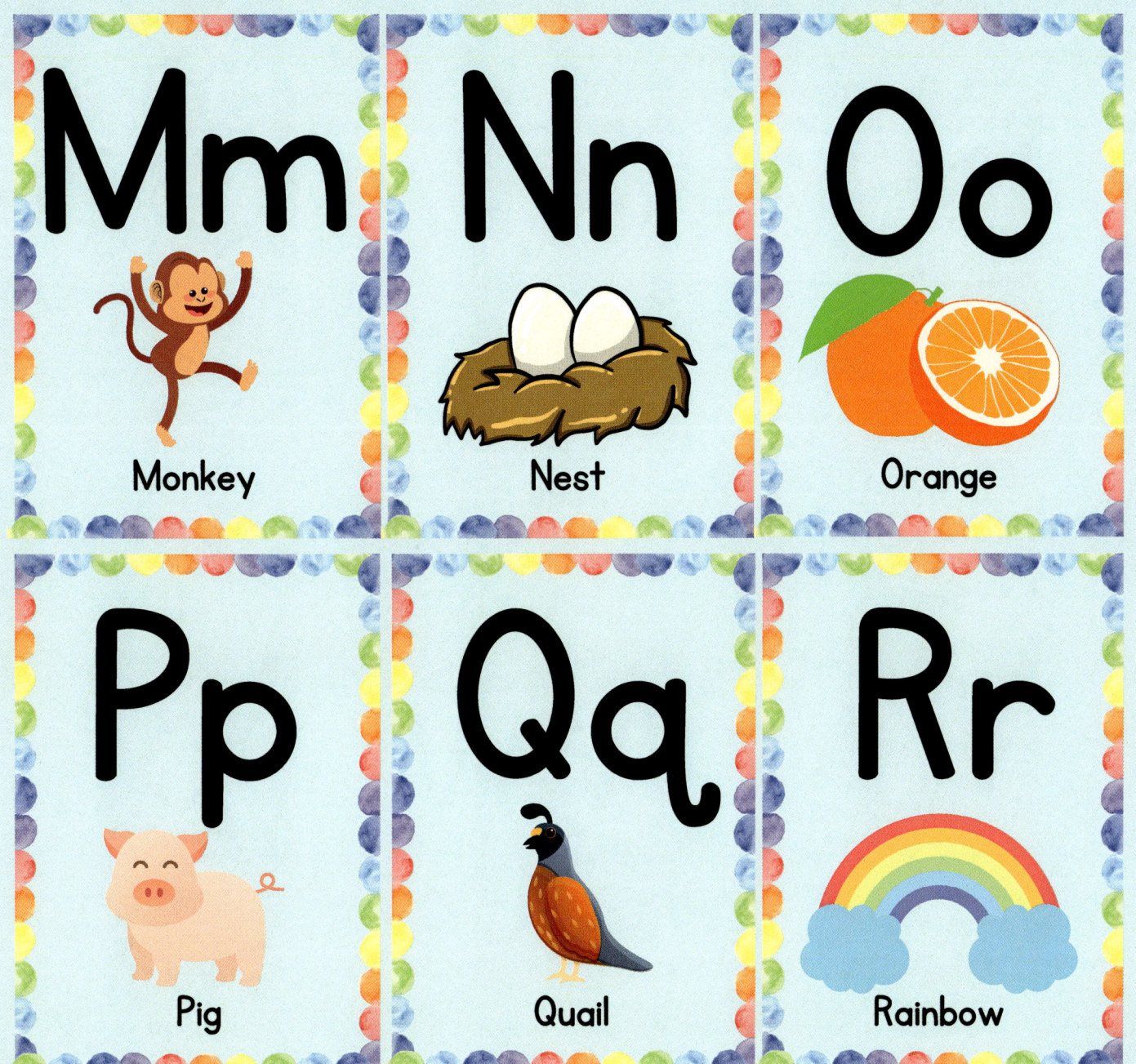

Ss

Snake

Tt

Tree

Uu

Umbrella

Vv

Violin

Ww

Watermelon

Xx
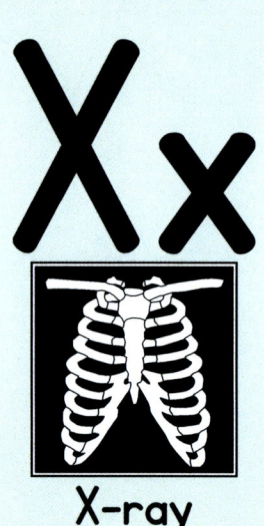
X-ray

Blending Words

Blending sounds to read words involves decoding letters into sounds and combining them to form a word. For example, a child who is proficient at blending would say: **/b/ /a/ /t/** ... **bat**. We will begin by combining two letter sounds, the consonant-vowel (CV) sounds, focusing on the initial two letters in three-letter words. In the subsequent section, we will explore three-letter words with the structure consonant-vowel-consonant (CVC).

Here is an example of this process using the word **bat**:

1. Identify the letter **b** and pronounce **/b/**.
2. Identify the letter **a** and pronounce **/a/**.
3. Run your finger slowly under the letters **ba** and pronounce **/ba/** slowly.
4. Swiftly run your finger under the letters **ba** and pronounce **/ba/** quickly.
5. Proceed to the letter **t** and pronounce **/t/**.
6. Run your finger slowly under the word **bat** and pronounce **/bat/** slowly.
7. Circle the word with your finger and say, **"The word is bat."**

Consonant Vowel (CV) Blending - Short Vowel Aa

Ask the child to blend the two letter sounds to create a word. For instance, the sounds of **/b/** in **ball** and **/a/** in **apple** blend to form **ba**. Encourage the child to repeat the blended sounds for approximately 10 seconds before moving on to the next two-letter blend.

/b/ /a/ → ba
/c/ /a/ → ca
/d/ /a/ → da
/f/ /a/ → fa
/g/ /a/ → ga
/h/ /a/ → ha
/j/ /a/ → ja
/l/ /a/ → la
/m/ /a/ → ma
/n/ /a/ → na

/p/ /a/ → pa
/qu/ /a/ → qua
/r/ /a/ → ra
/s/ /a/ → sa
/t/ /a/ → ta
/v/ /a/ → va
/w/ /a/ → wa
/y/ /a/ → ya
/z/ /a/ → za

Consonant Vowel Consonant (CVC) Blending - Short Vowel Aa

Instruct the child to pronounce the **/t/** in the word **tiger** and then combine it with the blended letters **ba** to create the word **bat**. Have them say the word **bat** aloud. Encourage them to practice this three-letter blend for approximately 10 seconds before proceeding to the next set of sounds.

/ba/	/t/	→	bat
/ca/	/n/	→	can
/da/	/d/	→	dad
/fa/	/t/	→	fat
/ga/	/p/	→	gap
/ha/	/t/	→	hat
/ja/	/m/	→	jam
/la/	/p/	→	lap
/ma/	/t/	→	mat
/na/	/p/	→	nap
/pa/	/n/	→	pan
/qua/	/ck/	→	quack
/ra/	/t/	→	rat
/sa/	/t/	→	sat
/ta/	/n/	→	tan
/va/	/n/	→	van
/wa/	/g/	→	wag
/ya/	/p/	→	yap
/za/	/p/	→	zap

Consonant Vowel (CV) Blending - Short Vowel Ee

Ask the child to blend the two letter sounds to create a word. For instance, the sounds of **/b/** in **ball** and **/e/** in **egg** blend to form **be**. Encourage the child to repeat the blended sounds for approximately 10 seconds before moving on to the next two-letter blend.

/b/	/e/	→	be
/d/	/e/	→	de
/f/	/e/	→	fe
/g/	/e/	→	ge
/h/	/e/	→	he
/j/	/e/	→	je
/k/	/e/	→	ke
/l/	/e/	→	le
/m/	/e/	→	me
/n/	/e/	→	ne

/p/	/e/	→	pe
/qu/	/e/	→	que
/r/	/e/	→	re
/s/	/e/	→	se
/t/	/e/	→	te
/v/	/e/	→	ve
/w/	/e/	→	we
/y/	/e/	→	ye
/z/	/e/	→	ze

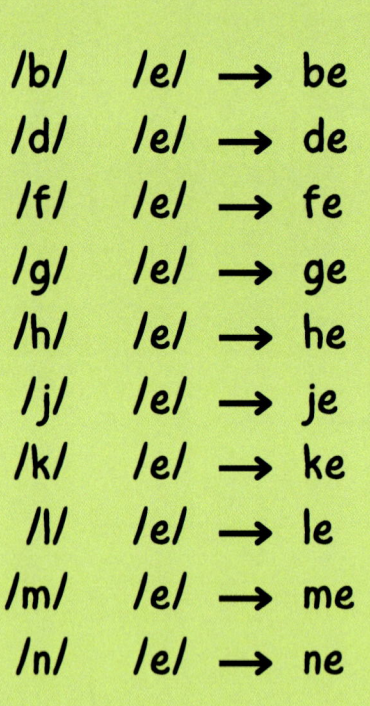

Consonant Vowel Consonant (CVC) Blending - Short Vowel Ee

Instruct the child to pronounce the **/t/** in the word **tiger** and then combine it with the blended letters **be** to create the word **bet**. Have them say the word **bet** aloud. Encourage them to practice this three-letter blend for approximately 10 seconds before proceeding to the next set of sounds.

/be/   /t/   → bet
/de/   /n/   → den
/e/   /nd/ → end
/fe/   /d/   → fed
/ge/   /t/   → get
/he/   /n/   → hen
/j/   /et/ → jet
/ke/   /n/   → ken
/le/   /g/   → leg
/me/   /t/   → met

/ne/   /t/   → net
/pe/   /n/   → pen
/que/ /st/ → quest
/re/   /d/   → red
/se/   /t/   → set
/te/   /n/   → ten
/ve/   /t/   → vet
/we/   /t/   → wet
/ye/   /t/   → yet
/ze/   /n/   → zen

22

Short /e/ Match

Draw a line to match the picture with the word.

 • • net

 • • ten

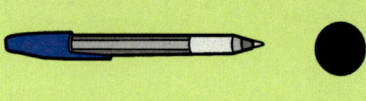 • • bed

 • • vet

 • • red

 • • pen

 • • web

Consonant Vowel (CV) Blending - Short Vowel Ii

Ask the child to blend the two letter sounds to create a word. For instance, the sounds of **/b/** in **ball** and **/i/** in **igloo** blend to form **bi**. Encourage the child to repeat the blended sounds for approximately 10 seconds before moving on to the next two-letter blend.

/b/ /i/ → bi
/d/ /i/ → di
/f/ /i/ → fi
/g/ /i/ → gi
/h/ /i/ → hi
/j/ /i/ → ji
/k/ /i/ → ki
/l/ /i/ → li
/m/ /i/ → mi
/n/ /i/ → ni

/p/ /i/ → pi
/qu/ /i/ → qui
/r/ /i/ → ri
/s/ /i/ → si
/t/ /i/ → ti
/v/ /i/ → vi
/w/ /i/ → wi
/y/ /i/ → yi
/z/ /i/ → zi

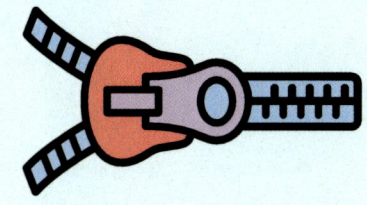

Consonant Vowel Consonant (CVC) Blending - Short Vowel Ii

Instruct the child to pronounce the **/t/** in the word **tiger** and then combine it with the blended letters **bi** to create the word **bit**. Have them say the word **bit** aloud. Encourage them to practice this three-letter blend for approximately 10 seconds before proceeding to the next set of sounds.

/bi/	/t/	→	bit
/di/	/p/	→	dip
/fi/	/t/	→	fit
/gi/	/g/	→	gig
/hi/	/t/	→	hit
/ji/	/m/	→	jim
/ki/	/t/	→	kit
/li/	/t/	→	lit
/mi/	/d/	→	mid

/ni/	/b/	→	nib
/pi/	/t/	→	pit
/qui/	/t/	→	quit
/ri/	/p/	→	rip
/si/	/t/	→	sit
/ti/	/p/	→	tip
/vi/	/d/	→	vid
/wi/	/n/	→	win
/yi/	/p/	→	yip
/zi/	/p/	→	zip

25

Short Ii
Write the Word

Use the word bank to help you write the word on the line.

  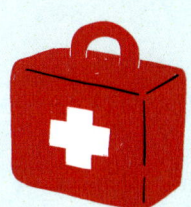

| win | dip | pig | kit | fin |
| dig | lid | wig | lip | |

Consonant Vowel (CV) Blending - Short Vowel Oo

Ask the child to blend the two letter sounds to create a word. For instance, the sounds of **/b/** in **ball** and **/o/** in **octopus** blend to form **bo**. Encourage the child to repeat the blended sounds for approximately 10 seconds before moving on to the next two-letter blend.

/b/ /o/ → bo
/c/ /o/ → co
/d/ /o/ → do
/f/ /o/ → fo
/g/ /o/ → go
/h/ /o/ → ho
/j/ /o/ → jo
/k/ /o/ → ko
/l/ /o/ → lo
/m/ /o/ → mo

/n/ /o/ → no
/o/ /x/ → ox
/p/ /o/ → po
/r/ /o/ → ro
/s/ /o/ → so
/t/ /o/ → to
/v/ /o/ → vo
/w/ /o/ → wo
/y/ /o/ → yo
/z/ /o/ → zo

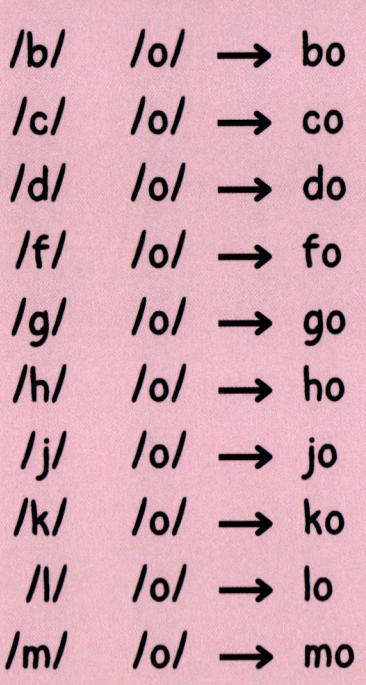

Consonant Vowel Consonant (CVC) Blending - Short Vowel Oo

Instruct the child to pronounce the /t/ in the word **tiger** and then combine it with the blended letters **bo** to create the word **bot**. Have them say the word **bot** aloud. Encourage them to practice this three-letter blend for approximately 10 seconds before proceeding to the next set of sounds.

/bo/	/t/	→	bot
/co/	/t/	→	cot
/do/	/t/	→	dot
/fo/	/g/	→	fog
/go/	/t/	→	got
/ho/	/t/	→	hot
/jo/	/g/	→	jog
/lo/	/g/	→	log
/mo/	/p/	→	mop

/no/	/t/	→	not
/po/	/t/	→	pot
/ro/	/t/	→	rot
/so/	/d/	→	sod
/to/	/p/	→	top
/wo/	/k/	→	wok
/yo/	/t/	→	yot
/zo/	/t/	→	zot

Say the words out loud. Color the pictures that have a short o sound.

Short Oo

mop

Circle the words with the short o sound.

not	jog	bed	lip	mop
cop	map	pot	sob	hat
hot	sad	cat	fog	cot

Write 4 words with the short o sound.

29

Consonant Vowel (CV) Blending - Short Vowel Uu

Ask the child to blend the two letter sounds to create a word. For instance, the sounds of **/b/** in **ball** and **/u/** in **umbrella** blend to form **bu.** Encourage the child to repeat the blended sounds for approximately 10 seconds before moving on to the next two-letter blend.

/b/ /u/ → bu
/c/ /u/ → cu
/d/ /u/ → du
/f/ /u/ → fu
/g/ /u/ → gu
/h/ /u/ → hu
/j/ /u/ → ju
/l/ /u/ → lu
/m/ /u/ → mu

/n/ /u/ → nu
/r/ /u/ → ru
/s/ /u/ → su
/t/ /u/ → tu
/v/ /u/ → vu
/w/ /u/ → wu
/y/ /u/ → yu
/z/ /u/ → zu

30

Consonant Vowel Consonant (CVC) Blending - Short Vowel Uu

Instruct the child to pronounce the **/t/** in the word **tiger** and then combine it with the blended letters **bu** to create the word **but.** Have them say the word **but** aloud. Encourage them to practice this three-letter blend for approximately 10 seconds before proceeding to the next set of sounds.

/bu/ /t/ → but
/cu/ /t/ → cut
/du/ /ck/ → duck
/fu/ /n/ → fun
/gu/ /m/ → gum
/hu/ /t/ → hut
/ju/ /g/ → jug
/lu/ /g/ → lug

/mu/ /g/ → mug
/nu/ /t/ → nut
/ru/ /n/ → run
/su/ /n/ → sun
/tu/ /b/ → tub
/vu/ /g/ → vug
/yu/ /m/ → yum
/zu/ /z/ → zuz

31

Short Uu Word Find

Read the words next to the picture. Color the correct word that goes with the picture.

32

Long Vowels

A long vowel is a term used for vowel sounds that are pronounced the same as the letter itself. Let's focus on the most common form of long vowels. You will notice a pattern in long vowel words: there is always a silent **e** at the end. This **e** goes by various names, like silent, magic, or bossy, but its function remains consistent.

Let's use the word **cake** as an example. In **cake,** the **e** at the end doesn't make a sound, but it tells the **a** to say its name. So, we say **cake.** The final **e** in a word signals the first vowel to sound out its own name.

Keep in mind, the vowels are AEIOU.

Long Aa Words

cape	hate	made
cane	rate	mate
safe	save	cave
gave	fate	fade

Write the Word
Long Vowel /a/

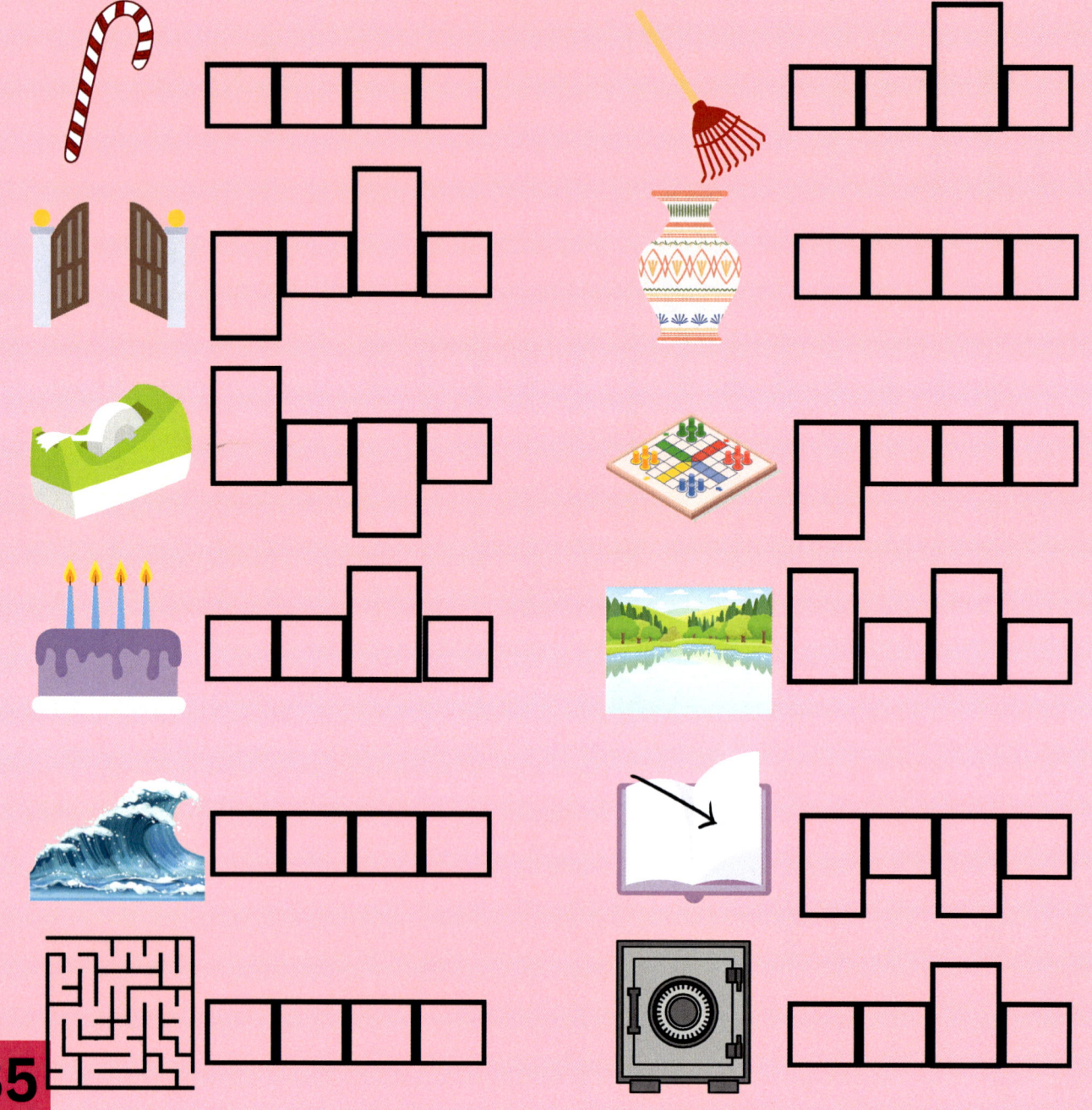

Long Ee Words

eve	gene	even
equal	mete	be
we	key	me
leo	pete	evil

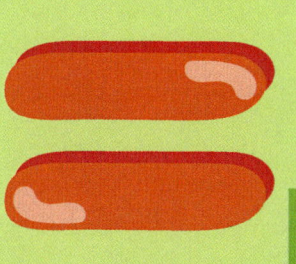

36

Long Vowel /e/

In the CVCE pattern (consonant-vowel-consonant-silent e), the letter e itself does not present with many words that fit inside of the pattern. There are always exceptions to rules.

In this activity, you will find words that make the long e sound at either the beginning or the end of the words.

E	G	O	L	E	S	H	Q	F	L
V	E	Q	T	S	Q	V	R	I	A
T	H	Z	T	E	F	U	V	K	A
Y	R	L	P	Q	B	E	A	E	M
Y	V	C	H	D	Q	W	V	L	X
G	Z	Z	L	B	L	E	B	K	V
I	D	I	U	P	N	T	Q	F	H
R	O	G	J	U	U	U	B	U	Q
E	D	E	Y	I	A	W	Y	P	T
U	T	S	S	O	A	E	K	L	N

BE   EGO   EQUAL   EVEN
EVIL   HE   WE

37

Long Ii Words

bite   fine   ice

site   fire   pine

kite   ripe   time

side   hide   vine

Long Vowel /i/

Read, Write, and Color

READ	WRITE	COLOR
time		
bike		
fire		
kite		
dime		
vine		

39

Long Oo Words

robe	tone	note
hope	code	cone
pope	bone	cope
zone	nose	vote

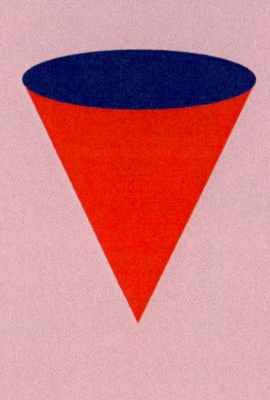

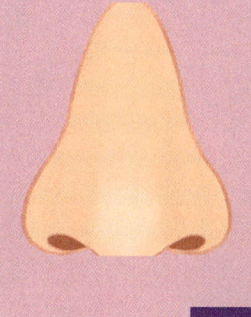

Long /o/

Color the picture. Then, finish writing the word and read it.

h _ m _   c _ n _   v _ t _

b _ n _   r _ p _   r _ b _

41

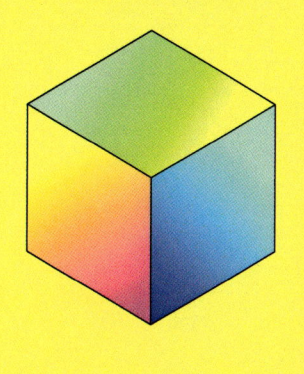

Long Uu Words

huge   cube   tube

cute   tune   mute

lute   june   fume

muse   dune   rule

Long /u/

Circle the word that matches the picture.

cube
cub

rud
rude

mut
mute

flut
flute

rul
rule

mule
mul

tube
tub

huge
hug

fume
fum

tun
tune

43

Comparing Short and Long Vowel Words

When comparing the sounds of short and long vowels, it's essential to understand their key differences. Short vowels are typically pronounced in a quick and concise manner, with a brief and sharp sound. Examples of words with short vowels include **cat, bed,** and **sit.**

On the other hand, long vowels are pronounced with an extended sound, lasting longer than short vowels. They are often represented by the same letter as their short counterpart but produce a different sound. Examples of long vowels can be found in words like **made, see,** and **go.**

Understanding the distinction between short and long vowels can significantly enhance the pronunciation and comprehension of words in the English language. Practice and repetition are essential in mastering the nuances of vowel sounds. On the next page are some comparisons between long and short vowels.

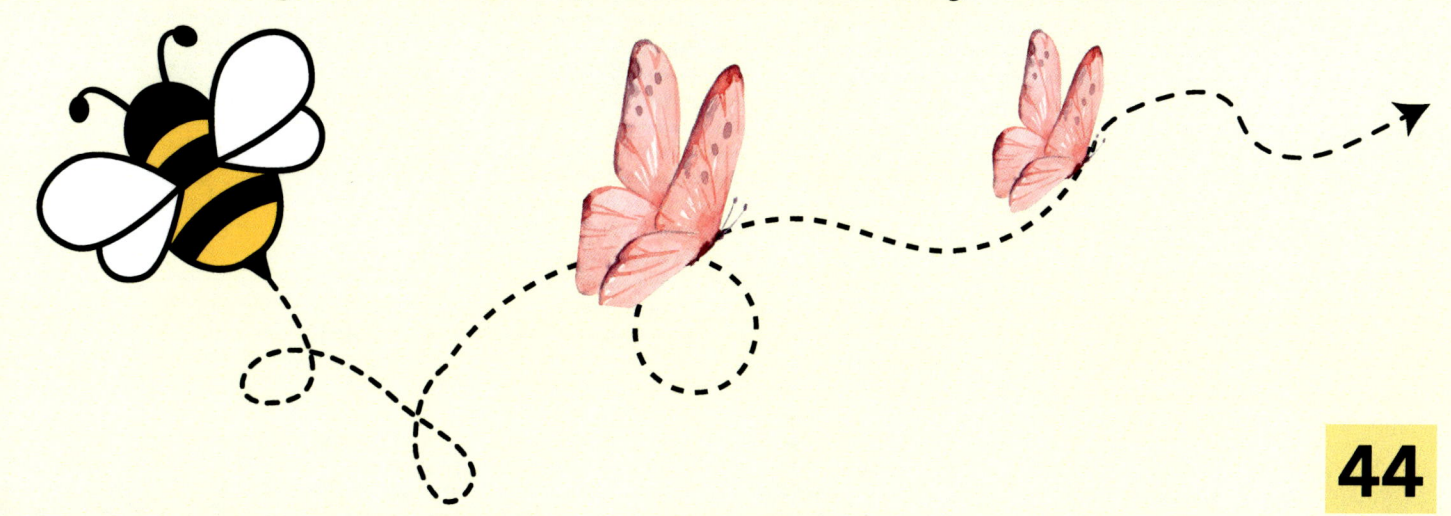

Long and Short Vowels

Short	Long	Short	Long	Short	Long
Cap	Cape	Bit	Bite	Hug	Huge
Cod	Code	Fin	Fine	Tub	Tube
Rat	Rate	Hid	Hide	Cub	Cube
Hat	Hate	Win	Wine	Kit	Kite
Mat	Mate	Con	Cone	Hop	Hope
Van	Vane	Rob	Robe	Mad	Made
Pet	Pete	Pop	Pope	Pan	Pane
Dim	Dime	Cut	Cute	Pin	Pine

Sight Words

Sight words are essential words that should be recognized immediately. These words are commonly found in books and everyday conversations and are fundamental for writing. They may not follow typical spelling patterns or be easily sounded out. Hence, they are sight words – children need to recognize them. Here is a list of common sight words to help kickstart your child's reading journey.

a	no	I	she	me
am	to	is	he	we
and	do	it	her	are
as	of	in	him	see
an	go	my	yes	for
all	be	up	but	had
so	got	if	did	was

Sight Words

not	the	after	why	like
out	then	from	who	only
had	they	help	were	come
you	them	went	when	some
your	there	have	what	that
with	here	gave	where	this
must	want	said	which	make

Missing Vowels

Fill in the missing vowel to make the word represented by the picture.

👄	l		p	🐱	c		t
🍓jam	j		m	☀️	s		n
🛏️	b		d	🍳	p		n
🧰	k		t	🥍	n		t
🦵	l		g	🗺️	m		p
🐕	d		g	🐷	p		g
🐭	r		t	🧹🪣	m		p
🐞	b		g	🖊️	p		n
🫁	r		b	🌰	n		t

48

CVC Word Puzzle

Arrange the jumbled letters to identify each object.

_ _ _	_ _ _	_ _ _
arc	bxo	tac

_ _ _	_ _ _	_ _ _
nbu	tne	xfo

_ _ _	_ _ _	_ _ _
ipn	sbu	pmo

Word Sort

Read each word out loud and sort it into the correct column.

hot   tune   cup   cave   eve   bike
lime sun   lake lip   game nose
bed   kit   dog   big   poke cube

Short Vowel Sound	Long Vowel Sound

Write the Word

Use the lines to help you write the word with long vowel sounds.

Hint: Don't forget that tricky letter at the end!